A Letter to A Lost Cause

By: Alexandra Lewis

For everyone that thinks they deserve to be on the dedication page,
but mostly for my Abuela.

HOW TO FEEL

Yearning for someone other than myself.
Someone that could teach me
how to feel.
How to make untouchable passion real.
To relish in a dying flame.
Someone to reignite.

I found you.
You taught me how to love you
And learn to
i hate myself.
I took the kindling from my fire and put it on yours.
Watched you burn the stars out of the night sky and
singe the hair from my arms
until the heat glare
was all I could see.
Until your distortion became
my reality.

POETRY

You were a metaphor.
A comparison without using "like" or "as"
because you were both
      like and as.
You were a verse,
      a free
verse,
without limit or   limitation.

You were a rhyme, playful
and tricky
like a jester with whiskey.
You were a stanza,

constructed your own beauty
out of
      nothing
but
Light.
You were epic,
like a poem
you had written
Only for me.

Memoir

I know your hand better
than my own history.
A distant memory
cracked skin and
antique palms,

I read them like a memoir.

They tell a lyric of your distant future.
Your fingers are history compared to
your bygone eyes.
Lashes flutter me
away and there's
nothing to remember
except the
     Midnight
that glows under your eyelids.

FLAMES

Your words were smoke.
thick, yet simple
impossible to inhale,
easy to digest.
They burn a hole through my chest.

You let them rise through my chimney and crackle
in the pit of my stomach.
I watched flames eat
forests like cereal for breakfast.
As I reached out to touch
Your magic,
your smoke
set a fire in my lungs.

Black night falls like a blanket

over a dusty sunset
stars
fill me with a bleak disdain from reality like the
sparkle of a
            dying wish,
a diamond necklace swinging
            back and, forth

grazing god's never ending skin.
wearing the universe---a silky soft dress.
You spin the Earth in Your boney fingers that roll
planets like marbles off rigid finger tips.
from this dewy grass i can not see
the godly thing that
enraptured You and me.

Your Playlist

Your melody was a hymn for my
stagnant soul.
Beating rhythm into my
tuneless bones and
singing sweet nothings,
That filled my empty head.

SUMMER STORM

I want to be your summer storm.
I want to build, like a
thunder symphony in your belly,
and rage through a watched, night sky
with winds that pull your roots from the ground.

I am the lightning.
Silent, with a
        thunderous illusion.
Struck
        three
                times
I am the whispering flame,
waiting to be blown out.
waiting
four
five
six seconds.
I am the waiting--

the violent waiting.
The impatience that makes your

hands shake
uncontrollably everytime you hear
my voice in the
distance.

TEA CUPS

In my dream of you
It rained warm ginger tea.
I stuck out my tongue
and savored each sweet drop.
Indulged in your liquid sunshine and
spun a spoon made of sugar
around the rim of your
scorching hot
tea cup.

SMILES

your smile reminds me of everything
I can not have.
standing on a rooftop, trying to touch a star,
nothing but empty promises and
prompt
rejection.

HONEY AND LEMON

Honey and Lemon.
Honey and lemon,
that's what she'd say as if those two words
could melt my problems away.
She'd feed it to me in silver star spoonfuls and
I'd lie back and wait for the nails in my throat to
dissipate.

Honey and Lemon.
What I praised on those mornings when
the only god alive was the one that
had teeth dripping with vengefulness.

Honey and Lemon,
the two things I knew would never fail me,
sweet like a bee and sour like the sting
Honey and Lemon
glued my heart back together like brick and
mortar.

Honey and Lemon
wiped the tears from my night sky eyes
like the manifestation of a tissue

Honey and Lemon.

Honey and Lemon, the only thing it couldn't fix
was
your hurricane.

You, were Honey
and Lemon

You made the pain slip away,
but let the morbid suffering
rot me from the inside out.

SUNBURNED

Sitting in the sun until it burns the
outer layer of our skin.
Until it tingles like a radiant frostbite.
A brilliant haze making sunflowers seem
Holy, resting in the sun.

It'll Pay Off In The End

I think I liked it.
The way you pushed me to the side,
corrosive chemicals in your lab.
You spilled me on your battered, sidewalk

tasteless gum.
All I remember is wishing I had enough flavor for
you.
Wishing that inch of pain you caused
with every demeaning joke
brought you some type of twisted joy.
But even after I gave you every ounce of sugar I
had,
I was never able to satisfy your sweet tooth.

SILENCE

I remember when you stopped talking to me.
I remember the fuzzy silence on the phone call, the
one that radiated
hatred after our fights subsided.
I remember interrupting you,
and the pause that fell in between the jumbled
words-
and then wait for one of us to start talking again.
I remember when you lost your voice.
When I realized my world was silent without your
thoughts
ringing in my head.
I remember the text I didn't read until hours later.
The one that made life not worth living.
Yelling, banging pots and pans with your words.
Smashing wine glasses on concrete.
My tears stained blood,
and all I wanted was silence.

I WANT

I want to live like I've never lived before
I want to breath crisp cold air until it burns the back
of my throat
I want to yell until my lungs collapse
I want to walk with such power that the earth
crumbles beneath my feet
I want to see the sky, looking through a crystal ball.

I want my skin to radiate energy,
To power thoughts envious like the moon of the
sun.
I want words sharper than knives.
Words that cut through tension like clouds.
Words that make tears fall purer than rain
Words thick like arsenic in her late husband's
martini.

I want hands that shape futures.
Hands that wrap around her glass
Like his hands wrapped around my shoulder.
Hands that choke the meaning out of life
And life out of body.

I want a body.
One that doesn't fight back when I run.

One that snaps necks and breaks backs.
One that claps back when
She laughs at my
Blistered back because she couldn't tell a
Hard worker from a gold digger.

I want a voice.
I want a booming soft voice.
One that lures men in like a siren
Then sinks their ships for the heck of it.
A voice that's louder than a gun
But more dangerous than an innocent dead man.

I want the world to sweep me off my feet
And take me home to the stars
Where everything we know means nothing.
Where my hands, my skin, my body, my voice.
Is nothing
but empty space.

shaking

Little white lies
are blind to the heartbeat
of a dying perspective.
A sensitive focus and personified
readiness,
wraps diamonds
around my tired eyes,
like skin to a dry bone.
Sucking the life out of
a drawn on cliche by day
and a sly rhyme by starry night.
What if all the riches in the world
could satisfy your needs.
Like poison you'll always regret letting
it takes advantage of you so easily.

How sweet of you to think of me
as I pass by on a summer's day
turned winter night
by your eyes;

White as snow,
glossy and empty
Severely   Unsteady,
I hold you.

Hoping my arms : your canes
would be enough
to silence the shake in your
step.
How was I to know, your
Quiver was endless.

Distraction

My heart beats continuously
making restless air
feel like thunderstorms.

Lightning loses its meaning.
I wish it would cease
beating so mercilessly
in my chest.

She only thinks for herself.
Pumping blood through my veins which
she conquered her own.
Sucking the crimson ocean from my
body
and leaving me empty.

Palms

The skin on the top and
bottom of my hand are sewn together at
one barely visible seam that
shines in fluorescent light
only when my palms are sweaty enough.

The drastic change between the
textures of my skin worked like
dark waves crashing upon
white sands
and the mole on my pointer finger
like a lighthouse summoning cracks,
like ships to an empty shore.

Muted skin has no feeling until
picked open and blood flows
like a crimson river from
a fault line in the desert that is my rough cracked
palm.
I've been told that each fingerprint is different,
that there are no two alike
and the same goes for palms,
the more I scratch the surface of my skin
the deeper the crevices dive into my flesh.

I am fascinated by the way my
desert palms repair themselves.
The way cells grab onto cells creating a
bridge of dark imperfection between
two masses of beautiful land.

There is no life in my palms,
but they hold the power to create it;
when balled in a fist around a skinny piece of
graphite,
great sands find a tiny oasis and for
a second,
just a second,   they allow life to grow

Skin Wrinkled

Skin wrinkles like withering time
and sand falls quick through
empty wine glasses.
Spectacles make pills look
larger and needles sting newborn arms
like aged bourbon scratching its way down a
battered throat.
There's nothing between me and time but sunlight.
No room for waiting or wondering who comes next.
Sand slipping through chubby fingers like
childsplay at the beach.
There's nothing between me and time but the moon
shine.
Nothing between me and time,
Me and you—,
but this shot glass.
The one holding poison, forcing it down my throat.
Holding on so tight the glass breaks,
Making drunk blood run races down sweaty palms.
Your face was glowing in the strawberry stars, but
Your eyes, they blurred over time.
The only thing you can see is my hand in yours.
Cradling your bony fingers until they put you to
sleep.

FAITH

Your words they stung like knives.
Your hands they bruised like rocks.
Your laugh was so deceiving
and Your nighttime wonder was lost.
You held my hand and told me,
at the count of three we'll leap,
but when we got there You let go.
I fell long and deep.
In that frosty water,
I crawled up on the sand.
The water filled my lungs, then
spilled upon the land.
Your army watched me bleed,
You stood there blank and
guilty,

i sat there and i softly cried.
Surrounded by Your lies.

"BAPTIZE ME"

Baptize me in waters that oceans can't cure.
Make me the Eve that Adam can endure.
I want the hand of God on my back,
maybe he can love me.
Or find someone that wants to take his place,
please hold me.
Teach me how to love again, Like I loved the one
that
broke my artist's hands.
Or maybe braid my hair with
grease that feels like home.

Baptize me in waters that make the future new.
That breaks my skull with bricks
of paper and purple glue.
Wash my hands with swear words
and find that soulless tune, the one that makes my
head hurt
the one with baby blue.
Keep me above the water,
just enough so I won't drown.
But just under the water line,
enough to hear
my desperate sounds.

Confessions to a New Relationship

He wrapped a rope like gold chain around my neck,
pulled back,
told me breathe,
My body rejected.
Carved lyrics into my palms
with ink like holy water
                    and prayed to god he'd give a
                    pretty Swine to slaughter.
The tears that made his eyes swell told me he meant
it
when he apologized for the lies
                    like wine they'd been
fermented
I think he needs to rethink his place in heaven
because hell's been waiting for a savior, and God
he's such a blessing.
I can't wait for the day he tells her the truth
looks her in the eyes and make sure she counts his
confessions,
what is he gonna do when she starts to question,
                    How daddy took the
pain from his wolf and became a shepherd?
Should I think of him when he puts his hands on me
around my throat it   burns
                    like fresh brewed tea.

and everytime he leaves it hurts a little less
his voice it soothes like shots fired
                    Numbing cream.
He had   thunder in his shoes
and   lighting in his breath
there was   oceans in his tears
 and poison   death in his head.
He taught me about the flower, and how her petals
grew.
but when he saw one growing he couldn't tell me
what to do.
He'll teach her about the berries, and Eve's
forbidden fruit.
one day he'll up and leave, just like he did to
you.
I forgot about his thunder, but he left a note stained
with a map of rivers,
and that note's all I have left, but his
daughter's   much less   bitter.

I dreamt that I could fly

Air whips past my ears
nothing but the
Whisper of a vengeful wind.

I dreamt that I could fly

From poison on a rooftop
I dreamt that hands could catch me,
That I was light as rain drops.

I dreamt that I could fly,
And fall, fast as diamonds.

I'd shatter on cold concrete and
Spread a million pieces.

I dreamt that I could fly,
Away from crimson rivers.

Fall flat into cotton covers
Tucked in for restful sleeping

I dreamt that I could fly
And land without a splatter

Fly right out my nighttime window,

Come back in sunlight's
Morning chatter.

Your Cage

I dried my thoughts like flowers.
I starved for thirty days
and thirty nights.
I bled and
bleed like a fountain.
I died over and over
until I got it right.
I walked a desert of fire and
peeled the skin back from my palms.
I chewed the glass you broke on the floor,
seasoned with blood and wine.
I prayed, a silly prayer and tore the
pages from your bible.
I fed you from a lions belly
and spilled blood like beer.

You stopped digging your own,
and dug my grave,
Lit my body on fire and watched my eyes
Turn to milk.
I freed you from your lion's cage
but when you saw the animal in my eyes,
you turned around
and locked me down
And in your cage I cried.

I think my shoes are tired

I think my shoes are tired
From running far and wide
I think my shoes are tired
From stomping out dusty hides

I think my shoes are tired
From walking days on end
I think my shoes are tired
From waiting for a friend

I think my shoes are tired
Rocks make holes in rubber soles
I think my shoes are tired
My laces tied through button holes

I think my shoes are tired
From swimming in the river
I think my shoes are tired
From gathering wedlock silver

I think my shoes are tired
Eaten away by hell
I think my shoes are tired
In the corner of my prison cell

I think my shoes are tired
Sitting on a wooden stair
I think my shoes are tired
Tucked beneath a deckchair

I think my shoes are tired
Laying on the floor
I think my shoes are tired
Kicking in heaven's door

REMEMBER ME

Sunlight dies and her eyes turn grey like stormy
skies.
Nothing left but time ticking away at a life that's
not there anymore.
Eating away, swallowing my name and replacing it
with one I don't recognize.
Turning her arms into canes, and silence into
delusions.

Nothing left but time, ticking away at a life that's
not there anymore.
making a mockery out of her smile,
turning her arms into canes, and silence into
delusions.
Humming songs that play like demons in her dizzy
head.

Making a mockery of her smile,
she stares back at me, blank, empty.
Humming songs that play like demons in her dizzy
head.
Lullabies that keep me up at night, promise me
you're not leaving.

She stares back at me, blank, empty.

Wishful dreaming, that the songs stop one day.
Lullabies that keep me up at night, promise me
you're not leaving
I can't live with your wishful dreaming.

I can't live with this heavy feeling
eating away, swallowing my name and replacing it
with one I don't recognize
please, remember me, as your
Sunlight dies and your eyes turn grey like stormy
skies.

She Moves

Her hips moved like molasses
and her cheeks, like powdered noses.
The words that left her mouth were
written in bold.
She had jars of poison, rattling in her eyes,
green like garden snakes
and with a look she could take
your last breathe and make you
Pray.

1/25/17

I wish the sun wasn't as bright as your eyes,
so I could stare into the sky and watch the
wind pushing clouds.
I want to see you fly in the birds,
The sunshine beaming down
dries the crystal dew off
of grassy plains.
I want to see you move with the trees,
with the breeze
Strong, but quiet.

Eternity

Maybe what I found was exactly what I was looking
for.
A sweater that held me tightly.
An untouched parcel, as he was.
I,
expecting an apology.
Apologize for the lies he used
to suck me
in and grow like weeds winding up
a forever growing tree, for me to spend
eternity trying to
cut down.

Shores

Waves crashing upon silent, waiting shores
Feet resting in wet, white, crackling sands and cold
red hands
Feel the wind blow and stop between her breaths
Green sea, fiery skies, like her eyes that grant me
life

Feet resting in wet, white, crackling sands and cold
red hands
Her smile stops time from turning day to night
Green sea, fiery skies, like her eyes that grant me
life
Beautiful, glistening on the sunlit ocean waves,
frozen in our time

Her smile stops time from turning day to night
Keeping the shadowy disapprovals at bay
Beautiful, glistening on the sunlit ocean waves,
frozen in our time
Teaching me how to fly far away from this land we
know

Keeping the shadowy disapprovals at bay
She parts the sea that was once drowning me

Teaching me how to fly far away from this land we
know
Loving me, showing me how the flames dance on
the ocean's shore

Her love sings so sweetly to my rhythmic heart
I feel the wind blow and stop between her breaths
She loves me like the ocean, her child, telling it to
move softly, quietly
Waves crashing upon silent, waiting shores

For S

I want to marry my shadow.
I knew it would come back home.
I don't have to sit
on the edge of my bed,
waiting for it to call.
We could dance tangled in beautiful,
moments.
Breath mints
could make up for the
ocean breath kisses.
We could sit close together,
softly whispering,
counting,
breathing,
Every exhale, slowly finding its way between my
eyelashes.
You could lay next to me and let your tears
roll down a white snowy mountain
puffy cheeks.
I could,

I wish we could run fast
through the trees and find the little log over the
creek.
You'd sit there and play.

I'd sit there and sing.
We'd walk back silently.
Leaving the music there to mix slowly with the
cricket songs.
Oh darling I wish you were my shadow,

Ephemeral

I know a place,
where thoughts are controlled by
antagonists,
and lovers are controlled by thoughts.
The sky is grey,
and you can walk across the thick brown ocean
waves.
The horizon burns with fire and
the ground is brittle. Fragile.
The plants do not grow there,
Neither do my lungs,
Filled with a thick rigid, solid air.
Fields of vines and tombstones are
loud with the silent
kneeling above the bruised bones.
And when the last one is spent, it'll be spent on the
ephemeral,
Just as it is,
Ephemeral.

Watch Me

I've been watching you
watch her
watch him.
Across the hall,
the room
the city,
your words,
a noisy void.
Walking on air
Hypnotized,
by her beautiful ignorance.
Falling into sweet sharp love,
like a knife
ready to kill.

11/12/17

Something so sickeningly sweet about the way you
speak,
and when you leave you take me with you.
My heart can't help but stay one beat behind yours,
and when we fight,
our voices tangled together
In anger, a forceful dance,

                that,

                      oh god,

when we stopped arguing in love,
I lost your voice,
the one thing that gave life to my tears.

Know Her

I want to know her.
              I watch the way she
                  walks with the world,
talks with her hands
Runs with the wind
                  trailing
                      behind her,
how she wipes the tears from her eyes
when she knows she's about to cry.
She likes her brown
              hair
              straight
but wants it to be curly.
Her eyes are dark like her eyebrows
and she looks down at her feet when she's nervous.
She has no fears,
Except for spiders.
She's all I want,

                  but I don't know her.

panic

There's an earthquake
in my leg
and a river in my palm.
My hair flies through the
air like fall leaves and
lashes surf through oceans of tears.
There is nothing left for me,
my nails picked and spread on the floor.
There is no time left for me here,
I think that's her
knocking on my spineless door.

Empty Your Pockets

You didn't have to hurt me the way you did;
Mercilessly

Starting conversations with no destination,
hoping they'll pick up in the middle and
build their own foundation.

I was hurting, you were pulling

Empty your pockets, and give me back my keys,
you don't need them
You never needed me

WAR

Welding words into swords making enemies
Regret evil doings.
Righting wrongs that make
 drifters find home under a
musty bridge.
War comes from my
argument between words and
My mother described it as,
The devil.
Wake up with it in the morning, sleep with it at
night.
It's painted against my eyelids and
tattooed in my skin.
Against a gun, my words are excalibur,
just another plastic sword in the end.
Everything strong bows down to
Youthful letters.

Patent #111702

I'm your pretty little fool and you've
Been doing a good job of fooling me.

Believing there was a god.
                              Praying prayers that were
coming back

Empty

           wondering if disappointment is the
           Only thing I'm capable of
feeling.

Born a sin in the hands of

                 perfection, God
is the one who's angry with me
For believing I could reach
Infinite possibilities.

That I was in control of my own destiny

That I could remove myself from this empty space

And discover something more

Tempting than hell

and more

Enticing than heaven.

sadness doesn't excuse your infidelities
if it did the world would be hell and

hell would

be empty.

God can't tell me when life begins
Or when it ends.
Neither can breath,

or air,
or man declaring

martial law
on my body.

My belief in being infinite
Without a god having to create it
is more terrifying to my mother than

Her own life,
Swaying like a pocket watch in the hands of her

God
Who

Would drop her to the pits of eternal
Damnation

before
She could wimper on her knees for forgiveness.

Having faith the size of a mustard seed
Is not all that I am capable of.

I want to experience something Godless.
An apostate,
a heathen.
I want to live in a world
Where being

humanistic
isn't mistaken for being

Impias.

To love without rules
To think freely without having to fear my eternity.
I want to own myself.

It's been awhile

Since the last time I wrote about you,
I found a new "you" to write about.
And they don't remind me of you,
But their hands do, when they hold mine.
Pruney fingers fight their way through my knotted
hair.
But they don't remind me of you.
I feel sick.
I can't tell whether it's because I miss having a
"you",
Or because I'm still sick of loving you,
But they're a different type of "you".
It's so lovely loving this new "you".

We went Swimming

Tilted

The way she walks in stagnant waters.

Her neck,
    Slanted.

      Rolling streams of
                 Ice water
                 down
          A
      snaking
spine

Pressed against
The
Skin
of a
Steady
Back.

The words roll
       off
          her tongue

Gleams of silver
Shining
Fish

Make their way around our

Rod-
like
legs.

Rooted in the sand,
Our ankles wrap kindly in the

dark

deep sea wrack.

The way the fish curved to a point,   sharpened and
                        separating.

I find,   I don't love her.

I never did.

I feel nothing, and felt nothing, and will feel .

Sun shines,
            and

she understand
the warmth of home in my arms

Warmth that I couldn't, can't, won't feel wrapped
in hers
she tells me

                                                "It
                                      feels like
                                      home"

She and I are
different.

I don't know what her home is supposed to feel
like.

The dying wood behind the stark white sheetrock
that
paralyzed me in my
        Dreams. This is home

I don't tell her that this is what home is supposed to
feel like.
She doesn't know
She doesn't   want   to know.

She doesn't   care

That her lack of interest shows a newfound

Shallowness
In a loveless relationship.

I don't despise her for thinking I'm what she
wanted

Just betrayed by the adrenaline that
Uprooted

Lies of Love
Shameless commitment

Bohemianism

I. Clouds. Magnificent
    Iron out the kinks in the trees that
    Line the shore.

II. The humming of the waves
    Matches her subtle breath.
    The distance distracts you
    From our lost connection

III. I see the outline of your eyelashes
     refract and refrain the glow from
     Your weary artist eye.

IV. I know you could never love me
    But the way your hair moves with the
    Grass makes me believe
    I'm worth loving.

V. You pace back and forth
    Crackling, fire, gravel.

VI. Laps of water on the begging shore
    the way the lightning loves to love you.

VII. Make me believe this swarm of gnats,

Around me
Are a sign of weary blossoming
apricot love.

VIII.   No rhyme
or reason
To why you make me feel powerless.

IX.   I myself am struck with
powerless lightning
disillusioned and plagued by
demented and delerious,
Eyes

XI.   Stop playing with your eyes.
Stop playing with my eyes.

XII.   Please don't let that gaze have been for
nothing
don't love me for me,
Love me for this moment

XIII.   Grow please, like the tide
Let your river eyes over run
Me with disappointing dreams.

XIV.   Let this moment be your last,

let me be your first.
let me let you question who you are.
let me let you believe you can be
something other than the summer tide
says you can be.

XV.   Be the rattle of the cicadas.
Humm me awake from our dream.

XVI.   The north star is the brightest thing I can see
from here,
    But you, you besides me.
    We are blinding.

XVII.   The lightning makes me think
that life may be worth living.

XVIII. Flash photography,
    You capture me
    All of me
    Holy.

XIX.   Night has begun, an
    Aphrodisiac for a soulless, Tuneless mind.

Broken Poem

Horror, may linger on,
in my case
no -sufficient cause.

The sights which I had seen,
of this feeling
my life
Beautiful :

Around me,
all
I loved;
she was beautiful

I,   I. I,   she
more precious
than the world.

Life without her?

what was life
But:
crushed
compared
Attention.

Could interfere
loathed them;
     I knew
         Knife in heart.

Existence intolerable., tender, soft
              tender
              trustful!
in listening
                      ,in wondering
        blessed
        bright
             tears in
        Loving
        heart
          "I see it all"

Tears Of Chiffon

Crush me like eggshell
mortar and pestle.
Grind my thoughts, fragile
Skin,
powder-
Turn my ivory bones
to cotton,
Soft in the center, your

        supple skin : cooked rice
alabaster hands
carve them into yours and

cover my body with

Tears of Chiffon

when
you lay me to rest
string me along threads
Of coconut milk lace
and tie me tight around your neck like my
        mothers pearls.
unable to breathe
Trapped in winter frost.

OIL

Words spill across her paper
       slick
              thick, oil
It wasn't poetry,
more like rain pouring from her mouth.
I slipped on her oil
       again
            again.
Pushing myself up off the rainbow ground
covering my hands, oil
       blackened
She continued

hysterical,
She laughed
She cried
hysterical.

Over her tears,
she pushed out more
Words.

Overflowing a still empty page
each time,
just escaping the

clutch of being forged from ink,
imprinted forever on paper.

She was cold,
Her eyes were a furnace.
Burning down our enchanted forest.
Here I stood,
I stand
On smoldering land,
Surrounded by the consequence of
Her oil spill.
I wish the pages had caught her words.

I wish, when your oil spilled,
It soaked your
      Violent
         Page
And spared me of your fire instead.

1:02 PM

As I sit here at 1:02 PM on a mundane tuesday afternoon, knowing I have three essays to write, a practice SAT to take, poems left hidden and unread, a book left unfinished and broken, my stomach empty and nervous, my head pounding and spinning, and spinning, and spinning in howling winds. I can see you looking at me through these pages. Wondering how much is left of me. How much you thought you knew. How much you still don't know. All the questions you're scared to ask me, which I probably don't have answers to myself. Maybe you're thinking about me differently. Maybe now I'm quiet for a reason. Maybe now you understand why I'm so bold. Maybe now you think one of these poems is about you. Maybe now you don't feel as close to me as you used to. Or maybe now you feel closer to me than you ever have before. Whatever the case, I didn't know how to end this. How to wrap up a piece of work with so many missing pieces fluttering around my head looking for a place to settle in this collage of fragmented thoughts. I opened with striking vulnerability, and now I will end with an amicable goodbye. Keep in touch.

Sincerely,

Alex.

Made in the USA
San Bernardino, CA
06 May 2020

70668255R00040